BACKLASH
PRESS

A pioneering publishing house dedicated to creating intelligent, vivid books.

Established to inform, educate,

entertain and provoke.

Journal Isolation

A Backlash Book
First published 2020

Backlash Press
71 Goldstone Crescent, Hove, England,
BN3 6LS

ISBN: 978-1-9162666-8-1

www.backlashpress.com
info@backlashpress.com

All rights reserved. No part of this publication may be reproduced, stored in a retrieval system or transmitted in any form or by any means, electronic, mechanical, photocopying, recording or otherwise, without permission of the copyright holder.

Copyright © Gretchen Heffernan 2020
The moral rights of the contributors have been asserted.

Designer:
The Scrutineer, Rachael Adams.
Fonts: Baskerville, Bree serif.
Printed and bound by IngramSpark

25, May, 2020

This collection is wholly unique to any that I've curated. The incomparable nature of the submissions I received certainly reflected the exceptional times we are living through. Some were handwritten. Many were from teenagers, children, elders, and mental health patients. All were raw, perfectly threadbare in their humanness, and pining for connectedness.

Although I couldn't possibly include every submission I received, I tried my best to create a true elucidation of the sheer range of voices, the people's voices, inside this chronicle of our time in isolation. I wanted to archive an authentic window in verse and I'm gratified with the result. In so many ways, shaping this journal both broke and mended my heart. I was humbly reminded of why, and for whom, I started this press. Thank you.

All proceeds go to Mind and Mental Health America.

Love from,

Backlash Press

Hillery Stone

Hazards After Dark

The mouse has left its tiny trail on the table,
pills of black along the woodgrain where it roved
all night, corpulent and dimple-
backed as a yam. There isn't much to be found
but you've sealed every hole in the house and now
it can't get out. *So unlike a mouse*
the exterminator says, circling the room.
He takes out his rubber cement
and lies down by the radiator. There was a time
before this house, miles of world
and not a thing of it yours. There were years
you ruined everything good
because the outcome was incalculable.
Now you remind yourself about the shortened life span
of an animal in captivity.
You nose around for hazards after dark—
faint odor, electric hum. Not a particular organism
or object in a specified circumstance
but the unseeable. The stealth
design. If you're going to break a hole in the wall
you've got to do it soon. They're drawing
in. The whole house is nearly the size
of your Queen Anne's walnut-top now, smooth
as a map, ringed with secrets of our genes
and ancient climate. When you can't find your body
it will be there at the end, posed
for equanimity, signing interminable forms.
Remembering the tastes of the outside.

Claire Scott

Shelter in Place
after The Second Coming by W. B. Yeats

Things fall apart, the center cannot hold
fish unschool, birds unflock, geese ungaggle
while we stay home with books and crossword puzzles
behind shuttered windows and locked doors
wearing gloves to get the mail
disinfecting packages delivered by Amazon
in an upside down topsy-turvy
back to front world

Does hope bow to hopelessness
will Darwin's finches fly apart
perhaps there are some of us who remember
the fallout shelters of the fifties
complete with telephone and toilet
selling like hotcakes along with guidelines
for keeping frightened neighbors away
recommending one handgun per person

Can we say never again
and keep communities intact with texting
FaceTiming, Zooming and emails
leaving tomato soup for old man Zach
an Ann Patchett novel for Mia
a set of checkers on Ezra's porch
so anarchy is never loosed upon
this confused, misguided, amazing, wonderful world

Footnote to Shelter in Place

So delighted the first week or two
no dentist telling me I have dry rot
or need a root canal
no eye doctor saying I need new glasses
and Glaucoma is just around the corner
no lunch with my why-are-we-still-friends
college roommate, who talks nonstop
about her pet hedgehog
and then I looked in the mirror
my hair frizzed out, banshee style
salons shuttered as nonessential
who decided this anyway
no one ever asked me
so I grab my best scissors
the ones I use to cut up chicken and
trim the Loropetalum
and I begin
not too bad, definitely an improvement
until I take a shower and realize
I have to start again, hack hack
hanks of hair fall on the table, the counter, the floor
much better, but each time I pass a mirror
I see another clump poking up or down or sideways
and I cut
until I am practically bald
only a pathetic clump here and there
won't need a haircut for months
a hundred dollars in the bank
if it ever opens

J.S.

Lockdown

The Devil is in the house today
We can't go to school.
The voices in mummy's head have taken charge –
Today the voices rule.
They hold mummy's hand through the chaos
But make us hold our breath.
The devil will get in –
                      Keep holding –
There's a ready-made bed
Call the paramedics,
As the water flows
Blood is as thin –
                      When the veins explode.

Gret Heffernan

Isolation

is living all of myself at once

and under examination of what I have created.

Children. Poems. Versions of story. A life, small, but mine.

We create or destroy. We create to destroy. We destroy to recreate.

The momentum of a force that exposes weak systems

mis-constructed for the protection of the whole.

Bodies, governmental and otherwise, all fractured,

my children look out at our world

collapsing beyond the window, ask

What Now?

Now, you find something to love

and you use it to threaten false ideas

of immunity. Now, you understand

that the virus has only revealed

the real infection

Renée Olander

Isolation & Mental Health amid COVID-19
for Carolyn Hodgson Meyers Rhode

Skies open where massive trunks came down, canopied shades,
Whole ecosystems gone, climate change.

We cancel the beach house, postpone offering her ashes to the ocean
Yes, we say, it's good she doesn't have to live through this.

Sporting homemade mask around town, I hear so many birds call,
Spring unfurls by minute, second: tulips, irises, lilies of the valley.

I try not to look at numbers more than once a day, avoid obsession:
How many times can the towers come down? Children

Already disoriented. Most health care workers being women,
Yesterday's Times reported a New York hospital emergency medical

Director's suicide: after surviving COVID-19, she went back to
battle and buckled. In photos she smiles clear-eyed.

Yesterday my fingers found themselves around oil pastels, coloring
Mandala sent by our local domestic violence shelter: who knew

Coloring calms anxiety, approaches meditation in benefits?
Don't drink yourself to death, I say, finishing off a bottle.

Grief-hewn, I slept through this morning's wee hour meteor shower
And Milky Way. Now I muster, shoot for gratitude, another day.

Darren C. Demaree

There is Fruit, But

I cannot see the orchard.
The lights are on. Nobody
is begging me to leave,

but nobody is happy that I am
still sitting in the same spot
I was an hour ago.

All the drugs keep us whole.
I dream of being a tether
caught up in the wind

& removed. Our beauty
repeats. I cannot ascend past
the third floor. There is fruit,

but I cannot see the orchard.
I am in awe of the bloom
I cannot obstruct. This

prestige of a time is not
a trick. We talk about the sea
amidst the fresh water.

We talk about the garden
while he hold the seeds.
We're not ready to bury any-

thing yet. My name is the same
as it was two months ago.

I had hoped for much more.

Janet Bing

Groundless

The recent storm was so intense
it stole our power for a day.

It also felled one giant tree.
Now all that's left, a desperate stump
whose roots point up
embracing chunks of sidewalk.

Its roots still hover in the air
like many of us now,
shaken from our tranquil lives,
grasping for those "normal" days
before fear and a virus blew away
our weak connection to the earth.

Claire Scott

New Gods Needed

Older gods dropping out of circulation like unread books
Gen-X and Gen-Z taking over, fresh faces choosing new gods
tired of fire and brimstone, a hell furnished by Dante
tired of rarified air stinking of deceit
tired of threadbare faith and unanswered prayers
electing new gods next November, check it out
real face to face gods who take notes and keep promises
not interested in the next life since this one needs serious work
God of Toilet Paper, of Pasta and Rice,
God of Face Masks and Rubber Gloves
Goddess of Day Care, God of Decent Haircuts
Goddess of Manicures and Soothing Massages
the ballot over two hundred pages, doubling by the second
you can pick as many as you like, the merrier the more
and yes, you can mail it in and no, you don't need a stamp

Essential Services

Grocery stores we all agree
provided they have vodka and TP
also pharmacies for condoms we will never use
but make us feel young again and attractive
that package of Trojans worth more
than weekly facials or years of therapy
fast food of every flavor, Libyan, Latvian,
Zambian, Bolivian, Vesuvian
who has time to cook at home
dog walkers and gardeners
house cleaners and car washes
but please not the gym
no sweaty planks and pushups
or hours on a spin bike going absolutely nowhere
while music pounds your pulse
certainly not the dentist who is threatening
a root canal, several crowns and a lawsuit
for biting his finger while he needled Novocaine
of course manicures and marijuana
waxing and hair coloring
critical to precarious self esteem
seamstresses to alter sweatpants
bulging at the seams
heaping plates to relieve the monotony
of sheltering in place
up to five meals a day
moving to six pretty soon
to keep our eyes off the future
our future

Elaine Fletcher Chapman

Shelter in Place: Day 49

The starlings landed in the labyrinth

picking through the weeds for food.

I noticed them yesterday in the early evening.

Shiny black feathers. Only six or seven.

And here they are again this morning.

I wake weary. Wonder how the day will unfold.

Waiting for the wildflowers I planted weeks ago

to grow and bloom. We are writing a story,

a variation of other stories. Told and untold.

There are thousands dead with no way to say

their farewells. No way to send blessings forward.

Our distances greater than ever. Our love deepened.

Our daily pleasures measured by these slight sightings

of birds arriving and departing in the yard.

Pandemic

All week my husband has been closing up

his mother's house, bringing home his father's plow,

her good china. She turns ninety-one next

week and doesn't understand his absence.

We are sheltered-in-place. Our children miles away.

I built a Sanctuary Garden in the back

and a labyrinth in the front. Every day, circle walking.

Planted Marigold seeds. The dog is confused by

our constant presence. And yesterday my brother called

from North Carolina so I could hear the whippoorwill

in his side yard. Later he sent a recording after I said

it been years since I heard one. And today our wedding

anniversary, looking at the photos in a different light:

holding each other close with no hesitation, no fear.

Renée Olander

Threading

Hunker on down, you with a home, lucky so far.
Telework, homeschool, Zoom, order online.
Sport your homemade mask around town,
Wash your hands. Don't panic. Don't bear arms.
Navigate between obsession and avoidance. Meditate.
Nap. Boost your immune system. *Eat blueberries.*
Tamp your rage, despair, grief: misogynist racist-in-chief,
Bloody country, Ms. Taylor, Mr. Arbery most recent
Casualties, among so many. *Don't sleep.* Mind
The crimes. Read. Plant seeds. Don't baby
Talk the children. *Get outside. Be kind,*
Consider kindergarten. Light candles for
So many, including neonatals slaughtered
In the maternity ward. *Not to be born at all is best*
Sophocles suggested. *Persist O Poet*, or
Some such Emerson said, overrating self-reliance.
This tangle sticks. Seek comic relief. Watch
The Daily Social Distancing Show, admire
The impish, dimpled, dead-serious host. Embrace
Contradiction. *Dwell in possibility. Feed*
The birds. Find sparkles in the Cheyenne River
And Oglala Sioux tribes' checkpoints: hail
Their survival, persistence, fight. *Channel peace.*

Megan Preston Elliott

Blue Light

I rise to blue light   searching
for a connection   hoping
for a pixel-perfect replacement

touch;
in its absence I feel clean   skin
scrubbed raw to rid it
of your   ghost

dry
in its absence it feels   lonely

time mutates here
slipping through my fingers like a wet fish

into the quiet I   cry
for the company I cannot find
behind my pocked-sized screen

I fall asleep to blue light   heavy-
eyed and dream in mashed-up images
of an alternate life

to blue light I rise

Distanced Dating

I know how this goes

a split second to decide
if you like the narrative conjured
up in your mind
from the images they chose to provide

superficial snippets of complicated lives

the stillness of it makes me queasy
we do not fall in love with static images
images are easily
cropped   copied   changed
people are not
images are ghosts
they are abstract ideas
that mutate with each passing voyeur

thrust into the digital uncertainty of
dating apps
images are imbued with
a false power
one that makes you believe
that you can feel the richness
of human connection
behind a screen

in truth
images are illusions

onto which we project our desires
and if we can shake off

the potent expectation
of the image
we will free up space
for the unpredictable
inexplicable randomness
that is falling in love

The Gift

Today, I wake up weary. My mind worn down by the monotony of these days. The quiet of the empty house is palpable. I am so drained trying to soak up human contact through a screen; it's like living off a diet consisting only of salty crisps – addictive, but it leaves me thirsty and malnourished. Yet still, when I wake, I roll over and the first thing I reach for is my phone. Hoping that this time the blue light will bring something different. Always yearning for more when it doesn't come. A fool's game.

I force myself out of bed and my brain gets to work planning every second of the day. Frustration strikes when I don't have the energy to make it through the interminable list. The one thing I haven't scheduled any time for is feeling. Stillness. I decide that I will sit down with a mug of warm tea by the window for a moment. With vacant eyes, I observe the trees dancing in the wind. I find it difficult to focus and eventually notice that I am scrolling through my phone again. I even lift the phone, point the camera at the trees and watch the rhythmic sway of the leaves through the screen. It feels like a bitesize version of living. Putting the phone away, I stare out the window once more. This time paying attention. When the wind picks up speed, the leaves are hurled along with it. They come together, clapping feverishly like a cheering crowd. It reminds me of living. I watch, mesmerised, as single leaves break free from their branches and cascade to the ground. I study the grooves in the bark on the trunks of the trees that stand so strong in contrast with the flailing leaves. A cluster of knots next to a bulge in one of the trees looks like a face. A set of bewildered eyes, a pointy nose and a mouth, turned up at the corners. My face mirrors the tree with a soft smile. I have finally arrived. I pay attention to the weight of my thighs against the spongy leather chair. The soft ground cradling my feet as they rest. The steady rhythm of my breath. How my chest expands as the air fills my lungs. As I allow my body to feel whatever it wants to feel, my cheeks become wet. I feel a lightness as the tears spill down my face and soak into my skin.

What a gift it is to be here in this moment. To be alive and well and safely sheltered somewhere I can call home. What a gift it is to feel. To allow myself the opportunity to acknowledge the aching in my heart and release some of the tension. To breathe in new energy and settle my mind. What a gift it is to watch the trees.

Arun Jeeto

Narcissus and Echo in Isolation During COVID-19

Lockdown hit me
like an emotional gut punch
to realise that my eternal flame
for Narcissus, has been put out
by his icy tongue.
He caresses the
sharp jawline given to him
from his mother Liriope, taking selfies
of his effeminate face and Cephissus-like
body in the bathroom.
I watch him
smile as people flood his
DMs begging to hook up with
him, or another shirtless selfie gets
over two million likes.
He doesn't respond
to the messages, which gives
me hope that he loves me,
now isolation feels less painful and
lonely, but he says—
"I love you"
to himself, flicking through recent
selfies on his phone, and I
can only repeat his cursed words,
his back faces me.
He ignores me
repeating his cursed words, as
if a serrated edge knife
impales my heart, while I bawl
myself out of existence.

Joanna Farnell

Lockdown

Light, light, come again.
Life is hard without you here.
It makes me smile when you appear.

Darkness makes my life seem bad.
And winter always makes me sad.
As light appears through open window
And shines off my face with much grace
I feel like my life in not a waste.

I love the light as it shines so bright
That makes me feel I can see again,
It lifts me up as I lay in bed
And it doesn't make me feel I wish I was dead.

I know that summer will come again
I'll carry on writing my thoughts with this pen
As the sun slowly drifts away
And I notice it's the end of day.

Hazel Ettridge

Saved

Snatched from the square holes of civilisation
Where round pegs face daily humiliation
Caught in the arms of social isolation
Where all shapes can dance and breathe

Lauren Ketley

Lockdown, Lockdown

A virus came upon the world,
By the name of COVID-19,
A silent noise, uncertainty breeze,
The world, it closes, us humans,
Learning to cope in small doses,
For many will feel they don't belong,
As they fear, deeply, what's now going on,
Mental health matters,
Please be there,
It takes a phone-call, that's all you need to spare,
Missing our loved ones, so very much,
But the virus, it's vicious, only takes one touch,
It's for the best,
We will get through,
When all of this is over, the world will be new,
We really appreciate, key workers so strong,
Looking after loved ones, for them, it must go on,
We are all behind them, we all show love,
Just know it's important, to pray, to god above,
Send a little prayer, for the ones it has hurt,
The ones we have lost,
The ones to come, It's all very sad.
But please remember the good times had,
When all of this is over, a light will shine,
To take away the dull, from this very hard time,
Flowers will blossom, babies will boom,
We all will reunite, business's will strive,
We will all be thankful, for being alive.

Henrietta Cliss

After Lockdown
Small Acts

                              keep us steady
keep minds calm when
we can't "carry on"
small acts, simple
walking a while
forcing a smile
until it feels true
forcing a smile
to face the doubt
to rest, renew
keep us steady
with small acts
from the heart,
small acts in
solidarity
even when we're
                            apart.

After Two Weeks in Lockdown
The Colour of Hope

shut eyes turned to the sun: vermillion
mellowed bruises under easing skin: plum
wan winter skies washed to spring: cerulean
aged photographs unveiling novel pasts: sepia
newly setting suns or days just begun: cerise
unruly gardens hosting the most shades eyes
can perceive: olive, sage, viridian, sea
blissful sleep on newly laundered linen:
all the colours in dreams.

After Three Weeks in Lockdown
Lost Thoughts

churn in the cistern
pit of my hazy lockdown brain
churn, churn, and churn with acidic
doubt that starts to burn them down to vapour
burn, burn, and burn scolding the
cushion of my skull
as the glint of what I
tried to think evaporates,
slides out of my mouth to condense
like soft spit on windowpanes,
devoid of any meaning or purpose.

Maddi Crease

Tied Behind Curtains

I am
Tied behind curtains,
Wrapped up in the folds of velvet,
Looking out of the window.
I am crying.
I'm unsure.
I can't quite pin it down,
Find out what emotion builds so high
It needs this release.
But I am.
Outside the window,
The world keeps on rolling,
Going through the paces of life and
This, my lifetime, this time,
Traps me away from it.
I tangle myself further in.
I want to be immersed in streets.
I want to be out in the world,
World at my feet,
Free.
I know it's for the best.
I don't want to get sick,
Nor do I want anyone else to be.
My obsessions suffocate.
More than these window shields.
I curse down corona.
My words are no godly command,
I cannot fell it with sound,
But it makes me feel better.
I just wanna feel better.

The tears have stopped rolling,
But the earth keeps on going,
This planet is ever-moving,
Even without bustling streets.
This is comfort, at least.

Henry Bladon

Days of Isolation

Staring out at empty streets
has always been normal,
even though she used to feel
it was a thing to be guilty about,
but now it seems okay
to enjoy the comforting
waves of solitude caused by
enforced sheltering.
So, from her isolation
she looks out
onto the world outside
where people are lonely together.

Rooftop Dancer

Alone in her personal world
ensconced in the magic of movement,
the rooftop dancer in silhouette
against the evening sky.
Grace and poise.
She may never know the lightness
she may never know the joy
that the image
radiates in my lonely heart.

Bubbles of Sound

Through my window,
bubbles of sound
bounce in beautiful
ways,
floating to wrap
my isolated soul
in a musical hug.

Dr. Serena Fox

Masque

I, so late, behind a mask and shield,
Fog my glasses with recycled breath,
Scarce aware our smiles no longer wield
A reassuring, mutely-offered sheath
To lief and liege, bolt upright in their beds.
There, strange masks, more a lifeline sealed
Around flared nostrils, heaving chests, bowed heads,
Force oxygen through tissues half-congealed.
Both counterpoint and joust, this viral mess.
Stay home, we cannot even start to treat.
Come in, too late, failed lungs under duress,
Heaven and earth might move, but in defeat.
Our ICU's become Schrödinger's box.
Each knight, sojourner; each one, paradox.

Bruce Bromley

Heart Hurt
Tell me we'll never get used to it.
Richard Siken, 2005

The boy didn't know what to do with sounds that entered his head and became something else. His parents would soon be caught in the glare of their weekly murder mystery, its theme a barrage of horns lingering too long on the tonic, the note of houses and pillows and safe spaces, before charging up a diminished fifth and arriving at the tritone, or what his music teacher called "our satanic interval": it bedeviled the consonance that any ear ached for, whose achievement told the body where it was. Moments earlier, the boy had listened to the square of front lawn between his bedroom and the den, where his parents made themselves into the drinks they couldn't let go of and were about to merge with a televised disaster story they'd survive. He'd heard a mockingbird stump through the grass, part its beak on an E that rang across the air, that slid down a major third and up one step, a mating call hovered over by the moon, incapable of calling back. The boy saw these notes dotted on a staff as if he weren't in bed but floating high above them, the mockingbird's tune overlaid with booming horns in a gob of scored pitches he didn't know how to disentangle. He thought of his younger brother coiling in a tight S on the other side of the oval rug that separated them, how sleep was his hunger for the womb that made him. The boy thought of his own head pulped by sound becoming sight. And then he watched an archway rise up from the floor between their beds, its white like wobbling smoke through which he found another place, its details failing to come clear. He tugged the covers over him and was on his belly when the touch came, a triplet of touches on his lower spine, made by what he'd never identify as a hand. In the morning, sitting up, he looked down at the once shelved books he shared with his brother flopped in a mound on the rug you couldn't see, clothes off their hangers and encircling them. This room, the boy knew, was in the middle of a turn into something else, when the turning stopped.

It comes to him that where we lie or stand or walk must be adjacent to where we think we're not. The lives we plot for ourselves or allow to be plotted for us, when anything else seems beyond imagining, interface with what many don't yet understand enough to entitle with a name. But otherness can be reached for, enacted in a single life's stretch, and it can spread.

Lightning Source UK Ltd.
Milton Keynes UK
UKHW010004210720
366887UK00001B/55